Secrets of the Rich
Proven Strategies for Wealth Accumulation

Table of Contents

Chapter 1. Introduction

Immerse yourself in an exhilarating adventure to the pinnacle of opulence with our Special Report, "Secrets of the Rich: Proven Strategies for Wealth Accumulation." This is no mundane dissertation on finance; instead, it navigates the fascinating labyrinth of wealth creation like never before. Explored within these pages are the secret maneuvers of the affluent, strategies refined over the ages, and innovative tactics designed to burgeon your fortune. These aren't the inaccessible concepts reserved for top-level economists; these are real-world, practical, and applicable techniques sanctioned by the wealthy elite. Wouldn't you love to take a joyous jaunt into the realm of millionaires and billionaires? If the prospect sends a tingling of anticipation coursing through you, then this Special Report is your golden ticket. Prepare to be captivated, informed, and abundantly, inspiringly rich!

Chapter 2. Deciphering the Wealth Mindset

The innate capability to generate wealth does not fall onto laps from the heavens above, but is a potpourri of attitude, habits, ideas, and strategies - all of which coalesce to form what we call the wealth mindset. If you were to peep into the cortex of a tycoon, you would observe this dynamic, fructiferous mindset at work. So, let's venture into this enigma and lay bare its nuts and bolts.

2.1. The Art of Positive Thinking

Amassing wealth begins with a positive mindset. There are scores of affluent individuals who would agree that their journey towards prosperity started with optimistic thinking. This is not a saccharine-coated theory, but a proven fact evidenced by the wealth accumulation history of the elites.

Positive thinking breeds resilience. Even in the face of multiple setbacks or failures, it's the courage to try 'one more time,' stimulated by positive thinking, that ultimately leads to success and, by extension, wealth.

Your mind is your personal sanctum, a powerful lighthouse capable of throwing beams of positive energy, enabling you to navigate stormy oceans of adversity. It is an engine rumbling with relentless optimism, pushing you towards every lucrative opportunity that may come your way.

2.2. Habits: The Building Blocks of Wealth

If generating wealth was a towering skyscraper, habits would be its solid foundation. What sets wealthy individuals apart is not just their innate talent or dynamic knowledge, but their day-to-day habits. From the Micro habits like reading, exercising, and continuous learning, to the Macro ones such as strategic planning, networking, and time management - all contribute significantly to the wide landscape of wealth creation.

2.3. The Power of Continuous Learning

Wealthy individuals are voracious readers. They make it a habit to perpetually feed their brain with new information, insights, and ideas. This powerful habit keeps them ahead of the competition.

As Warren Buffett famously said, "The more you learn, the more you earn." They don't see education as a mere accumulation of degrees or certifications, but rather, as a ceaseless journey of knowledge acquisition. This constant learning helps them to identify, understand, and seize new wealth-generating opportunities.

2.4. Networking: Your Personal Wealth Multiplier

Without networking, the wealth mindset is like a weapon without ammunition. Mooching around in solace will not open up the portals of wealth. Wealthy individuals recognize networking as indubitably a critical aspect of wealth creation.

They see every person they meet as a potential ally who could open the doors to new opportunities, provide fresh perspectives, or spark innovative ideas. They imbibe it as a part of their daily routine. Networking could lead to the formation of profitable partnerships, significant investments, or key business relationships — each of which acts as steps on the ladder of wealth.

2.5. Strategic Planning: Charting the Course To Wealth

Another salient feature of the wealth mindset is strategic planning. Wealthy individuals don't just jump into things; they plan, and then they act. Every step they take is deliberated, every decision calculated, and every action measured to ascertain alignment with their long-term vision of wealth creation.

Proactive planning reduces the margin for error and maximizes success probability. Moreover, it helps them remain prepared for potential setbacks and capitalize on opportunistic sweet spots, thereby escalating their wealth accumulation pace.

2.6. The Power of Delayed Gratification

Possibly the least glamorous aspect of wealth creation is the art of delayed gratification. Wealthy individuals exercise strong self-discipline to seize the massive payoffs that come their way in the future. They understand the fleeting nature of instant gratification and the long-lasting benefits of compounding. They willingly forego short-term pleasures for their long-term financial vision.

Winning the wealth game requires playing by long timelines. It demands the patience to ride the waves, both high and low, and the foresight to sow seeds today for a bountiful harvest in the future.

2.7. Leveraging Debt: The Wealthy Way

Not all debt is bad. Wealthy people understand this and hence, leverage debt to grow their wealth. They use debt as a tool to finance their income-generating assets like real estate and investments. They see it as a stepping stone towards accelerating their financial goals.

While the masses grapple with the negative implications of debt, the affluent understand that the responsible and strategic use of debt can significantly amplify wealth and financial independence.

So, turn the page with a firm intent to overhaul your cognitive structures. It's time to fabricate your wealth mindset, the fulcrum upon which pivots the colossal structure of wealth generation. The road might be arduous, the voyage might be long, but the shrine of wealth is glorious and worthwhile. Harness the power of your mind, and make your active participant in this exhilarating journey of wealth accumulation. The secrets of the rich are now yours to grasp and implement. Venture forth with confidence, conviction, and a wealth mindset.

Chapter 3. Pathways to Prosperity: Passive and Active Income Streams

Passive income is the engine that drives wealth accumulation. It is money earned with minimal activity through a variety of ventures which require little daily effort or upkeep. The concept is a staple among the financially independent and wealthy. On the other hand, active income refers to income received from performing a service, including wages, tips, salaries, commissions, and income from businesses in which there is material participation. In this discussion, we'll delve in-depth into both income streams, offering you the direction to elevate your wealth creation journey.

3.1. Understanding Passive Income

Passive income involves earning money from a venture in which a person is not actively involved. A common misperception is that passive income requires no work. There is indeed work involved - it is just front-loaded. The setting up phase entails a lot of work, but once things start rolling, the requirement for active participation lessens dramatically, although may not completely disappear.

Real Estate Investing

A classic example of passive income is real estate investing. Rental income from a real estate investment is a quintessential type of passive income. It can be possible to passively manage properties by hiring a property management firm. Despite their fees, you can still collect passive income from your investment.

Dividends and Interest Income

Other avenues for passive income include dividends from stocks, where companies distribute a part of their earnings or reserves to shareholders, or interest income from money lending activities, providing a constant flow of cash with minimal effort.

Peer-to-Peer Lending

Another high-yielding passive income source is peer-to-peer lending, a form of crowdlending, where singles or groups of investors provide loans to other individuals or small businesses for profit. The profitability mostly arises from the interest rates earned on those loans.

3.2. Pathways to Active Income

Contrary to passive income, active income refers to income for which services have been performed. This is the sphere of salaries, wages, tips, commissions, and income from a trade or business.

Traditional Employment

The most common example of active income is receiving a wage or salary from a job. You trade your time and skills for money. The inherently limited nature of time restricts the overall potential of this income stream - there are only so many hours in a day to work.

Freelancing or Consulting

Freelancing or consulting is another type of active income. You can start a freelance gig in virtually any profession. Freelancing gives you flexibility and the potential to earn more than a traditional job in some cases.

Starting a Business

Starting a business is not just a pathway to wealth; it's a way to pursue your passion and fulfil your entrepreneurial dream. While it often involves an up-front investment and lots of hard work, a successful business can substantially uplift your income.

To enthrall yourself in the journey towards opulence, one needs to understand the power of blending both streams of income. Not only does diversification strengthen income security, but it also opens up opportunities for exponential wealth growth. Consider the potential of reinvesting passive income gains into active investments. Simultaneously, redirecting surpluses from active income to generate further passive income creates a robust and resilient economic environment that empowers you.

3.3. The Harmonious Dance of Passive and Active Income

A strategic blend of active and passive income has the potential to accelerate your wealth creation journey. It allows you to take advantage of both immediate gains from your active income and long-term compounding benefits from your passive income.

The key is finding the right balance for yourself, factoring in your life goals, risk tolerance, time availability, and unique skill sets. Fortune favors the bold, and the bold know how to dance harmoniously between the active and passive income streams.

3.4. The Opulent Outcome: Wealth Accumulation

As you navigate through your wealth accumulation journey, internalize the power of both passive and active income. Understand them as mechanisms to propel your fortune. Your balanced approach towards both will immensely drive your financial journey, leading you towards the land of grand prosperity.

Remember the mantra – 'earn actively, invest passively.' As you act on this framework, you'll find wealth accumulation less of a struggle and more of a strategic game. Your financial acumen will deepen, and your wealth will flourish in the garden you've so diligently nurtured.

Let this be the start of your captivating exploration into the provocative world of wealth- a journey postmarked with victories, strewn with knowledge, and speckled with the joys of success.

Prepare yourself to embrace the world of millionaires and billionaires, as this journey equips you with the skills to join their league. To the path of opulence trodden by the affluent, let us march forth, heads held high, knowing our fortune is in our control. Henceforth, your wealth story is no longer written by the whims of predicaments, but wisely guided by the strategy you've learned of balancing active and passive income streams.

Chapter 4. The Art of Successful Investing

All the world's great investors share one common trait: they see the markets as a game of chess, where strategic planning, rigorous analysis, and judicious patience pay off magnificently, not as a roulette wheel where fortune favors the foolish.

4.1. The Importance of Due Diligence

The cornerstone of successful investment is due diligence. This involves meticulously researching a potential investment, understanding its mechanics, its history, its competitive landscape, what drives its value, and potential risks. One must scrutinize publicly available financial reports, analyst reviews, and pertinent news articles.

Often overlooked and yet incredibly critical is the study of the company's management team. Are they experienced and competent? Can they navigate the company through thick and thin?

4.2. Understanding Market Mechanics

Markets are affected by a multitude of factors, with global events, industry trends, and even traders' psychology playing significant roles. Therefore, an investor needs to keep a watchful eye on the news, developing a sense of the market's direction and sentiment. This involves following both financial news and global events, considering trends, and developing a general understanding of economics.

4.3. Diversification: Don't Put All Your Eggs in One Basket

Seasoned investors spread out their investments across various assets types and sectors to mitigate risk. This strategy, called diversification, can dramatically reduce the possibility of significant losses. Champions in this game always have a diverse portfolio that can withstand market volatility and industry-specific downturns. Note, however, that diversification does not guarantee profits or protect against losses in declining markets.

4.4. The Power of Compounding

Although it may seem dull, compounding—earning interest on interest—is one of the most potent wealth accumulation tools. By reinvesting the earning from an investment, and thereby earning return on the return, over time, an investor can significantly multiply his or her wealth. The beauty of compounding lies not in the seeking of quick wins, but in recognizing the magnificent potential of slow and consistent returns.

4.5. Patience Is Golden

The greatest investor of our times, Warren Buffett, once said, "The stock market is a device for transferring money from the impatient to the patient." Those who aim for overnight riches often end up hemorrhaging money. Successful investing requires patience and the ability to resist the allure of quick profits.

4.6. Regular Investments: A Steady Approach

Regular investments, often through a plan like Dollar-Cost Averaging (DCA), helps mitigate the risk of market volatility. By consistently investing a fixed amount of money at regular intervals, one can purchase more shares when prices are low and fewer when prices are high. This strategy results in an average cost over time, potentially reducing the risk of investing a large amount in a single investment at the wrong time.

4.7. Managing Risk and Reward

Understanding risk and reward is fundamental for every investor. High-risk investments could potentially lead to higher returns, but they could also result in significant losses. Therefore, one must consider their risk tolerance before making any investment. Mitigating risks does not mean avoiding it entirely; it simply means investing wisely to balance potential profits and losses, often through portfolio diversification.

4.8. Deciphering Financial Reports

Financial reports such as income statements, balance sheets, and cash flow statements supply critical insight into a company's health. Understanding these statements helps in evaluating the company's profitability, its assets and liabilities, and its cash generation capability, assisting in making an informed investment decision.

4.9. The Role of Emotions in Investing

Investing could often stir up strong emotions, primarily fear and greed, which could lead to poor decisions. It's crucial to maintain emotional neutrality, making rational decisions based on solid research and facts, and not getting swayed by market rumors, hype, or panic.

4.10. Sustainable Investing: Profit with a Purpose

Increasingly, investors are eyeing sustainable or ESG (Environmental, Social, Governance) investments as a method to generate returns while contributing positively to society and environment. Such investments consider factors beyond the financial performance, thus aligning the investments with the investor's ethical and moral values.

These strategies collectively lay a solid foundation for the art of successful investing. However, remember that investing inherently involves risk and potential loss of principal. No strategy guarantees success. Hence, frequent self-education, following market trends, doing due diligence, and consult with financial advisors are crucial for every investor. In the magnificent journey towards wealth accumulation, remember that it's not just about the destination, but also about the lessons learned along the way.

Chapter 5. The Power of Financial Literacy

Underestimating the value of financial literacy is akin to traversing a path in the dark without a torch. It is an indispensable tool for carving a trajectory toward financial independence. Let's delve into the varied aspects of financial literacy that make up its vast terrain.

5.1. The Basics of Budgeting

Financial literacy commences with an understanding of budgeting. Knowing where your money comes from and where it heads is crucial to wealth accumulation. A well-defined budget acts as a financial roadmap, guiding your spending and saving decisions.

To begin, list your sources of income, including salary, businesses, investments, and any other cash inflows. Next, record your expenses--- housing, groceries, utility bills, entertainment, and so forth. The ultimate purpose is to ensure that income surpasses expenses. This surplus becomes the seed of your savings, investments, and rapid wealth accumulation.

===Understanding Savings and Investments

Having made a surplus through efficient budgeting, the next step is to comprehend the significance of savings and wise investing.

Savings provide a financial safety net, cushioning against unforeseen events. A dime saved is indeed a dollar earned. Begin by setting aside at least 20% of your income, gradually ramping up the percentage.

Investment, on the other hand, allows you to grow these savings. By finding opportunities that yield returns in excess of inflation and taxes, you wield financial growth's magic wand. Stocks, bonds, real estate, and mutual funds are the cornerstone of savvy investments.

5.2. The Power of Compounding

Imagine a snowball rolling down a hill. It gains momentum with every inch, growing larger and faster because of the accumulated snow. This is the magic of compounding, an essential principle of wealth creation.

Starting early enables your wealth to grow exponentially due to the power of compounding. Even modest amounts invested regularly can mound into significant wealth over time.

5.3. Managing Credit and Debt

Being wealthy is not merely about earning and investing money but also about managing debts efficiently. Financial literacy embraces understanding the cost of borrowing and the importance of a good credit score. Knowing when to leverage debt to your advantage, such as for investments with high returns, and when to avoid it, is a skill that can make or break your financial journey.

5.4. Financial Planning and Retirement

Planning is the navigator in your wealth journey. A solid financial plan, one that takes care of short-term and long-term goals, aids with decision-making regarding investments, insurance, savings, and estate planning.

Retirement planning, too, deserves special mention. Being rich is not just about living a life of luxury today but also about securing your golden years. Contribute generously to your retirement fund and draw a retirement plan that ensures a steady flow of income when you stop working.

5.5. Insurance: Protecting Your Wealth

Insurance safeguards your wealth in the face of unexpected calamities. Health insurance, life insurance, homeowner's insurance, and auto insurance protect your financial resources, ensuring that an untoward event doesn't derail your journey toward extravagant wealth.

5.6. Taxes: A Pillar to Understand

Last but certainly not least, understanding taxation is crucial. Tax laws offer numerous strategies to save and grow your money. by employing legal tax-saving mechanisms, you can not only ensure the right contribution to society but also preserve your wealth.

In the final analysis, financial literacy is a crucial skill in our endeavor toward wealth accumulation. It is, indeed, the difference between living life and living it well! By exploring budgeting, savings, compounding, credit management, financial planning, insurance, and taxes, we glean invaluable insights into how the rich stay rich and grow their wealth. So, proceed with an eager heart, an intent mind, and you will surely master the art of wealth accumulation!

Chapter 6. Wise Estate Planning for Wealth Preservation

Today, we commence our exploration on the crucial subject of estate planning - the quintessential method for preserving wealth. Many discern the term 'estate planning' as a dry, complex discourse, but it's quite the contrary. Picture it as a highly effective strategy in your arsenal for wealth accumulation and distribution that will secure your financial legacy in the long run.

6.1. Understanding Estate Planning

Broadly, estate planning implies how an individual's wealth is distributed after their demise. It encompasses a range of aspects: money, investments, real estate, and other assets, but isn't entirely about tangible properties. In essence, it's crafting a blueprint that defines how your wealth is allotted and to whom it finds its way, with the added consideration for the tax system. A well-orchestrated estate plan ensures that your resources are utilized and distributed according to your desires, thus preventing potential disputes upon your passing.

Estate planning is not exclusive to the super-rich. Irrespective of the magnitude of your wealth, it is crucial to erect a well-designed estate plan, lest your assets fall into unintended hands or, worse, become the subject of courtroom battles.

6.2. The Art of Will Crafting

Creating a will is a fundamental and initial step in estate planning. A will, in simple words, documents your directives regarding how the assets should be distributed after your death. Any individual above the age of eighteen, of sound mind can write a will.

A testament or will must be specific and comprehensive, laying out precise instructions on asset division. When writing a will, ensure that you've included all major assets and clearly specified allotment among your beneficiaries. Wills can also contain instructions about your last rites or the guardianship of your minor children. Consulting a legal advisor during this course could help prevent any ambiguity which could lead to conflict later.

6.3. Trusts: An Instrument for Minimizing Estate Taxes

Trusts, an often overlooked entity in estate planning, are instrumental in wealth preservation. A trust is an agreement that allows a third party (trustee) to hold and manage assets on behalf of the beneficiary.

Trusts can be utilized to limit estate taxes, providing for a smoother transfer of assets. A correctly set-up trust can bypass probate, leading to quick distribution of assets to the beneficiaries.

There are several types of trusts — revocable, irrevocable, asset protection, charitable, and generation-skipping trusts. Each serves a distinct purpose and has its own perks, costs, and tax implications. Hence, determining the optimum trust structure could import substantial benefits.

6.4. Getting Life Insurance

Life insurance is essentially a contract between the insured and insurer, where the insured pays premiums in return for the insurer's commitment to compensating the insured's beneficiaries upon the insured's demise. This sum, called a death benefit, is a vital aspect of estate planning as it offers financial sustenance to the beneficiaries.

Life insurance also proves beneficial in covering any pending debts or taxes and can provide a safety net should the family's breadwinner perish prematurely. Selecting the right insurance plan necessitates comprehensive comparisons of policies, considering the premium, coverage, and various other factors.

6.5. Building a Power of Attorney

A Power of Attorney (POA) is a legal document that grants a person or organization the authority to manage your affairs if you are unable to do so. These might include managing financial transactions, making medical decisions, buying life insurance, operating business interests, and so on.

Crafting a POA is a detailed process, requiring specific choices about who will stand in your stead, their purview, and the extent of their power. As several types of POAs are available, tailored to various situations and responsibilities, selecting the appropriate one is vital.

6.6. Ensuring Regular Update of Your Estate Plan

Updating your estate plan regularly, to reflect your present financial status and relationships, is vital. Key life events like marriage, divorce, birth of a child, death of a beneficiary, acquisition or selling of a substantial asset are moments that necessitate a review and potential adjustment of your estate plan.

In conclusion, estate planning is much more than simply writing a will; it is a complex process involving various legal documents, each serving a distinct purpose. It enables you to make well-considered decisions about distributing your assets. However complex it may seem, the peace of mind that comes from knowing your wealth will eventually find its way as per your wishes, is invaluable. It's not just about preserving your wealth but also about leaving a legacy.

Chapter 7. Diversification: The Golden Rule of Wealth Accumulation

Riding the thriving notes of success, we now find ourselves at a pillar that upholds the grand architecture of wealth acquisition - Diversification. Often encapsulated in the phrase, "Don't put all your eggs in one basket," diversification embodies a timeless wisdom woven intricately into the tapestry of wealth generation.

7.1. Forms of Diversification

Diversification is not a one-dimensional concept, cast in stone, and shrouded in the fog of financial jargon. It is a multidimensional, dynamic strategy that can be applied across various forms:

1. **Asset Class Diversification:** This involves spreading your investments across different classes such as equities, bonds, real estate, commodities, etc. Asset class variance provides a layer of protection as these assets rarely move in sync, softening the downside risk.

2. **Geographic Diversification:** It implies not restricting investments to a particular geography or country. Spreading them globally reduces the risk linked to economic slumps, political instability, or natural disasters in one region.

3. **Sector Diversification:** This involves not being tied down to one specific industry or sector. Different industries react differently to market cycles; therefore, varied sector investments increase the likelihood of weathering the ebbs and flows.

4. **Time-Based Diversification:** Also known as dollar-cost averaging, it entails spreading investment buying over a period

to mitigate market fluctuations.

Understanding these different forms, let's delve into understanding the rationale behind diversification.

7.2. The Rationale of Diversification

To survive and prosper in the unpredictable waves of the economic sea, a solid defense is as critical as an aggressive offense. Here, diversification plays dual roles: a protective sea wall against the stormy markets and a widescale net to catch the bounty of the economic ocean.

From the perspective of risk management, diversification cushions against severe losses. Assets in the portfolio don't always move in unison - a drop in one can be offset by a rise in another. This interplay amongst assets effectively lowers volatility, creating a more stable and less hazardous investment journey.

From the growth lens, diversification broadens the horizon, bringing non-correlated assets together to construct an investment portfolio that harnesses the growth of different sectors, markets, asset classes. Thus, it paves the way for balanced growth rather than reliant on one 'hero' asset.

But diversification isn't a magical elixir. Let's avoid the pitfall of expecting it to deliver high returns or completely eliminate risk. It optimizes returns for a given level of risk, smoothing the ride towards financial prosperity.

7.3. The Strategy of Diversification

Diversifying is not blindly purchasing varied investments. To harness its true potential, one needs a method to the seeming madness. Here's a step-by-step approach:

1. **Understand Your Risk Appetite:** Begin by understanding how much risk you are comfortable taking. This is highly personal and depends on your financial goals, age, income level and overall financial situation.

2. **Asset Allocation:** Based on your risk tolerance, allocate assets proportionally. The mix of equities, bonds, commodities, etc. depends entirely on your investment horizon and desired risk-to-return ratio. Younger investors often opt for a higher equity allocation due to their longer investment horizon and higher risk tolerance.

3. **Choose Diverse Investments:** Within each asset class, choose a mix that spans different sectors, geographies, and sizes. Don't forget, each asset class, region, and sector has its own risk-return profile, and this mixture should align with your overall objectives.

4. **Regular Rebalancing:** Revisit and adjust your portfolio periodically. Over time, some assets may outperform others, leading to an unintended concentration. Rebalancing ensures that your portfolio remains in line with your original asset allocation.

7.4. The Pitfalls to Avoid

While diversification is beneficial, one must beware of common snares, such as over-diversification. Owning too many different investments may negate the benefits of diversification and make portfolio management a Herculean labor. Not every investment is necessary, and your portfolio needs only but sufficient diversity to spread the risk.

Further, diversification is not a 'set it and forget it' strategy. Regular reviewing and rebalancing, as highlighted earlier, are integral to maintain the portfolio's alignment with your risk tolerance and financial goals.

Sailing through the sea of wealth accumulation, diversification is the seasoned mariner's compass. It steers us clear from stormy market downturns and guides us towards the sunny shores of financial growth. While it requires tactful application and diligent maintenance, the journey towards abundant prosperity is smoother and more secure under its guidance. Here's to embarking on the next facet of your exciting wealth accumulation endeavor with diversification, your reliable and insightful guide!

Chapter 8. Billionaire Habits that Fuel Fortune

To truly understand billionaire habits, one must first comprehend that being a billionaire is about more than amassing wealth; it's about thriving. It involves extensive knowledge of finance and economics, unparalleled tolerance for risk, relentless dedication to achieving goals, and a ceaseless quest for innovation. Unraveling the complex tapestry of these habits, it's our mission to inject you with the highest potency of financial wisdom. Let's begin our intriguing journey.

8.1. The Ritual of Early Rising

Rising early is a surprisingly common habit among billionaires, it seems simple, but it's a potent strategy that can give you a headstart on the day's events. The idea is to work on yourself or your business while the world is still asleep. Early risers like Richard Branson, Tim Cook, and Elon Musk use these quiet hours to read, exercise, plan their days, or work on their passion projects.

8.2. Efficient Time Management

Money may be the metric by which billionaires' wealth is measured, but time is the asset they value most. They understand that time, unlike money, cannot be earned back. Exceptionally successful people manage their time exceedingly well, often delegating tasks to others, so they can focus on what they do best.

8.3. Relentless Pursuit of Knowledge

Billionaires are often voracious readers and continuous learners.

They understand that the world is in a state of constant flux, and by devouring literature and brushing up on industry trends, they ensure that their knowledge base evolves with the changing dynamics. Case in point, Bill Gates reads around 50 books a year to satisfy his thirst for knowledge.

8.4. Embracing What's Uncomfortable

Billionaires understand that enduring discomfort is a precursor to massive success. Stepping outside of one's comfort zone enables an individual to take calculated risks and make bold moves that can lead to unprecedented growth. They often view failure not as a setback, but as an opportunity to learn and grow.

8.5. Regular Exercise and Healthy Eating

Physical fitness often correlates with mental resilience, and many billionaires swear by the impact of healthy habits on their professional success. Regular exercise and balanced meals not only promote longevity but also ensure mental sharpness, energy, and a sense of overall well-being.

8.6. Emphasis on Networking

Many billionaires acknowledge that their wealth is partly attributed to the people they know. Investing time and energy in building a network can open up myriad opportunities. They understand the importance of building a diverse network of people who possess different skills, ideas, and perspectives.

8.7. Prudent Risk-Taking

Billionaires know that risk-taking is a crucial component of wealth creation. While the risk propensity varies among individuals, all successful entrepreneurs take calculated risks to capitalize on the right opportunities.

8.8. Prioritizing Financial Literacy

The rich understand the mechanics of money better than most. They prioritize financial literacy, understanding complex financial concepts, investment strategies, taxation, and more. This knowledge guides their investment decisions, reducing the likelihood of financial mistakes.

8.9. Philanthropy and Giving Back

Philanthropy is deeply ingrained in billionaire culture. Giving back is not only an ethical imperative for many billionaires but also a testament to their belief in the greater good. Their generous contributions often aim to empower others to make their own wealth.

8.10. Mentoring and Being Mentored

Billionaires value mentorship greatly. They seek advice from those who've been there and done that, and willingly enlighten others who look up to them, creating a virtuous cycle of knowledge sharing.

Learning from the habits of billionaires can provide invaluable insights into the mindset that fuels wealth accumulation. Emulating these habits won't guarantee that you'll become a billionaire, but they can certainly set you on the path to financial prosperity.

Chapter 9. Striking Gold in Real Estate

Breathtaking vistas, majestic features, and the sheer magnitude of the tangible - such is the allure of real estate. More than simple bricks and mortar, real estate represents the very palpable and raw essence of wealth. Legends have been forged, legacies created, and dynasties sustained using the power of real estate. Engaging with this sector unearths a rich vein of opportunity promising not just returns, but life-altering wealth - if only one knows where to strike that proverbial pickaxe.

9.1. The Beating Heart of Real Estate

In real estate, location reigns supreme. Visions of plush penthouses atop urban skyscrapers or sprawling estates nestled in verdant countryside miss a vital point. Take a step back from these captivating images and understand that the true beating heart of real estate is not in the scale of luxury it affords, but in its location. Understanding this can mean the difference between mediocrity and unimaginable wealth.

Burgeoning cities, evolving neighborhoods, architectural trends, and projections of commercial growth - these are all key participants in the location ballet that dances in the realm of real estate. Tracking these patterns can result in advantageous investment decisions. Unearth cities on the brink of an economic surge and neighborhoods about to bloom due to strategic infrastructure investments; these are the hidden gems of location scouting that yield the most lucrative returns.

9.2. The Secret Sauce: Compound Effect

Compound interest is magic; compound effect is divine. When applied to real estate, this effect multiplies value exponentially due to appreciation, rental returns, and leveraging.

Appreciation, simply the increasing value of your property, is possibly the most delightful aspect of real estate. That charming cottage you bought at a quaint countryside price might well become a sought-after mansion when urbanization waves its magic wand. Ride this wave and watch your investment balloon from thousands to millions.

Rental returns or yield, another important factor to consider, paint vibrant pictures of a periodic cash influx. While it may start as a modest trickle, the compound effect, when combined with appreciation, transforms it into a tangible river of regular income.

Leveraging allows you to borrow capital to invest more in real estate, magnifying your ability to acquire wealth. Let's say you take a loan to buy a property. Tax advantages, rental income, and appreciation ensure that the returns far outweigh the cost of the loan. This is the beauty of leveraging. Not only does it propel wealth creation, but also provides a safety net in the form of real assets.

9.3. The Artful Tactics of Negotiation

Negotiation is an art more than a science, and therefore, it requires an artist's touch. It's about understanding people, their motives, their fears, and their aspirations. More importantly, it's about creating common ground where you both feel victorious.

Know the value of what is being traded, master the power of silence and the impact of the right information played at the right time. Show empathy, and let the other person know you understand their perspective. Above all, know when and how to close.

In the realm of real estate, negotiate not only for lower prices but also for better terms. This extends towards mortgage interest rates, approval processes, closing costs, and more. A single percentage point, when compounded, can make a difference of thousands, even millions, in the long run.

9.4. Real Estate Moguls Didn't Just Buy Properties—They Built Communities

The flashiest headlines shout about real estate billionaires and their opulent mansions but fail to capture the essence of their strategy. The real estate moguls didn't just buy properties, they built communities.

In building communities, real estate magnates don't just sell houses — they sell lifestyles. From urban dwelling, to countryside retreats, from active adult communities to excelling school districts, they understood the desires of their clientele and offered them that on a silver platter, hence burgeoning their wealth.

Think about it – when you buy property, what are you truly buying? Location, specific features, or a particular lifestyle? This is the art of selling dreams. This is how real estate moguls strike their gold.

More than just a transaction, wealth creation in real estate leans heavily on the foundation of trust. Conceptualizing value in the form of a potential community, envisioning spaces that nourish life, laughter, and growth, and realizing those visions - this is the crux of transforming square footage into gold.

Engaging with the world of real estate is, therefore, not just about accumulating wealth, but fundamentally concerns connecting with people, understanding shifting landscapes, bare-knuckle negotiations, and most importantly, building communities. The art of striking gold in real estate lies in the blend of concrete practices and more ethereal concepts, a blend you are now privy to. Only with these insights can you truly begin to flex your muscles in the world of real estate, each move taking you closer, ever closer, to the pinnacle of wealth.

Chapter 10. Blueprints to Business Mastery: The Entrepreneurship Route

The road to wealth via entrepreneurship is undoubtedly a challenging one, yet its potential rewards are substantial, creating an unparalleled level of financial and personal independence. It eliminates the restrictions of a regular job and sets free the limitless potential of passion and purpose in your life.

In gazing upon the vast commercial landscape, we discern the outlines of an ever-shifting blizzard of possibilities. To navigate with clarity and precision through this tangle calls for a profound understanding of what molds an effective entrepreneur and a successful enterprise.

In this vein, let's unpack the blueprints of business mastery, revealing the relentless wit, wisdom, and willpower that have enabled several entrepreneurs to carve out their fortunes.

10.1. The Entrepreneurs' Mindset

At the genesis of every prosperous venture, there is an agile, innovative mindset. This mindset is not innate; it is cultivated over time. It necessitates an intrinsic motivation, unwavering mission and the willingness to risk and to learn from failure. Often, it is this ability to see the silver lining in situations most would consider utterly hopeless that sets apart the truly successful entrepreneurs.

To adopt this mindset, immerse yourself in a world of self-improvement and growth. Devour books on business, listen to podcasts by successful people in your industry, research business trends and technologies. A constant desire to learn, and subsequently adapt, is the key here.

10.2. Thoughtful Goal Setting

It's not enough to merely desire a successful business; this desire must be crystallized into tangible, achievable goals. Set both short-term and long-term goals with clear, measurable objectives. This adds a layer of accountability and gives you a road map to follow.

Remember, though, that practicality is king; setting impossible goals only promotes disappointment and inhibits progress. The goals should stretch and challenge you, but they also need to be achievable. Use the SMART (Specific, Measurable, Achievable, Relevant, and Time-bound) method for creating effective goals.

10.3. Producing a Robust Business Plan

A business plan serves as a formal statement of your business goals, detailing the reasons why they are attainable and your strategies for achieving them. The process of creating a business plan demands an intensive analysis of market conditions, competition, and potential risks.

A viable business plan should include an executive summary, a company description, an overview of your products or services, a clear outline of your marketing and sales strategy, and a specific financial plan. Such a business plan provides not only a vehicle for seeking financing but also acts as a guide for the establishment and operation of your enterprise.

10.4. Building a Resilient Corporate Culture

A strong, value-driven culture is a powerful boon for any business, adding a level of cohesion and facilitating the alignment of personal and organizational goals. The creation of such a culture begins with defining the core values and mission of your business.

Building a resilient corporate culture is a long-term commitment that necessitates time and consistent efforts. It requires regular revisiting of these values, reinforcing them in day-to-day operational decisions, and ensuring they are reflected in the actions of each team member.

10.5. Harnessing Innovation and Technology

Innovation and technology often serve as powerful catalysts for business growth. To harness their power, ensure you regularly evaluate emerging technologies for potential adoption. Software tools for customer relationship management, project management, and others can drastically enhance your productivity and operational efficiency.

Innovation is not only about adopting technology. It also involves thinking creatively about solving problems and improving processes within your business. Encouraging this sort of innovation across all levels of your company can be a potent driver of growth.

10.6. Building and Leveraging Network

The adage "It's not what you know, but who you know," rings especially true in business. A robust professional network can expedite your business growth through partnerships, mentorships, or simply by broadening the reach of your company's visibility.

Networking isn't only about attending events and swapping business cards. It's about fostering relationships by providing value to those in your network. Be generous in sharing your expertise, make introductions when appropriate, and always look for ways to help others in your circle.

10.7. Resilience and Perseverance

Every successful entrepreneur will tell you that their journey wasn't a straight shot to success. It was riddled with failures, rejections, and obstructions that threatened to derail their ventures. The common denominator among these successful individuals is resilience and grit. They don't see failure as a stop sign but as a detour or a stepping stone to success.

It's vital to stay the course in the pursuit of your business goals. Adapt your strategies when necessary. Learn from your mistakes, but never let them distract you from your ultimate objectives.

As we conclude this examination of entrepreneurship as a wealth accumulation strategy, do bear in mind that no two journeys are the same and that these are not iron-clad rules, but guidance distilled from the experiences of others. Tailor these concepts to fit your unique context, and you too can master the art and science of entrepreneurship.

Chapter 11. Securing your Financial Future: Retirement and Beyond

The journey to securing your financial future is a complex, intricate, and ongoing process. To ensure comfort and ease in your silver years, this chapter lays out a detailed roadmap.

11.1. Crafting Your Financial Vision

First, you must articulate a clear financial vision for your retirement and beyond. Picture your ideal retired life - your desired lifestyle, passions you want to pursue, and any financial commitments that may persist. It could range from globetrotting to cultivating a garden, supporting a charity, or bequeathing your wealth to your heirs. Translating this vision into monthly income will provide a tangible retirement savings goal. Use a retirement calculator for this, considering factors like inflation, expected lifespan, and potential healthcare costs.

11.2. Prioritize Saving and Investment

Your vision should serve as a beacon for your saving and investing strategies. Prioritizing saving requires discipline, but it is equally important to ensure that your money works for you. Allocate a portion of your income monthly towards retirement savings. Vehicle like 401(k) or IRAs provides tax advantages, automatically deducts contributions from your income, and some employers match a portion of your contribution.

Next, engage in a regular investment strategy. Investing in a diversified portfolio ensures not only the security of your capital but can significantly increase your wealth over the long term. Navigating the world of investments can be intimidating, but using managed funds or employing the services of a financial advisor can simplify the process.

11.3. Financial Planning and Wealth Protection

Effective tax planning is crucial. Regular review of your tax strategies ensures maximization of your wealth. Again, leveraging tax-advantaged retirement accounts, making tax-efficient investments, and gifting can provide tangible benefits.

Insurance is a pivotal element within wealth protection. Apart from generally recommended health and property insurance, consider long-term care insurance, given the skyrocketing costs of healthcare. An umbrella policy offers protection against large liability claims or judgements.

11.4. Estate Planning

Estate planning is an often-overlooked part of securing a financial future. A carefully crafted estate plan ensures that your assets are passed on to your beneficiaries as per your wishes, and it minimizes any tax liabilities. Wills and trusts are popular tools used in estate planning. It is vital to regularly update your estate plan as your financial situation and legislation changes.

11.5. Making use of Financial Professionals

Financial planning demands expertise and can be time-consuming. Engaging financial professionals like a financial planner, an tax advisor or an estate attorney can help ensure optimal decisions are made. Find professionals who understand your financial vision and can guide you accordingly.

11.6. Transition to Retirement

The transition to retirement is often a paradigm shift. Converting your savings into a retirement income demands a different approach. Annuities can provide a guaranteed income, while a balanced portfolio can give you a regular income as well.

Taking a phased approach to retirement, like consulting or part-time work, can both ease the transition and provide an income stream. Social Security benefits are a significant income source for many retirees, so it's crucial to understand when and how to claim them.

Your retirement years offer an opportunity to enjoy the results of your financial planning, but it is vital to continue monitoring and adjusting your strategies. Regular review of your investments, estate plan, and tax strategies keep you on top of any changes and ensure that your wealth lasts.

In conclusion, securing your financial future is not a one-time act or a linear process. It involves constantly adjusting and adapting to the changing financial landscapes, personal circumstances, and future dreams. Through a holistic approach to financial planning - balancing savings, investments, tax strategies, and estate planning - you can enjoy a comfortable and satisfying retirement and beyond.

www.ingramcontent.com/pod-product-compliance
Lightning Source LLC
Chambersburg PA
CBHW072219290526
45794CB00007B/2811